LOVE

is

like a *Tree*

For Frankie
– Shona Innes

For my Mum, Ruben and Andi
– Írisz Agócs

FIVE MILE

Five Mile, an imprint of
Bonnier Publishing Australia
Level 6, 534 Church Street,
Richmond, Victoria 3121
www.fivemile.com.au

First published 2017
Printed in China 5 4 3 2

LOVE
is
like a *Tree*

Shona Innes * Írisz Agócs

FIVE MILE

Love is a special and growing thing.
When you love something or someone who
is with you, you can feel so very happy.

You might feel like dancing or singing

or climbing to the highest
spot to shout out to the
world about your love.

Love is a little bit like a tree.
Love is like your own special magical tree that
you can climb up into, nest comfortably in its big
branches, and safely watch the world go by.

Like trees, love can come in different shapes and sizes.

There is the love you have
for things –

like the love you have for ice-cream
or spaghetti,

your books

or your toys.

There is the love you have for your friends
at school or in your sports team.

There is the love two grown-ups
have for each other –

like the love they have when they
want to move in and share the
rest of their lives together.

There is the love you might have for family —

like the love you have for your mum or your dad.
Or the love you might have for brothers or sisters.

Like a tree, love can grow and grow.
You can have your favourite spot in your
beautiful tree and still have room to share
it with someone else.

You can share plenty of your love and there will
still be more room left to love other people.

Like other growing things, love needs to be
looked after to keep it growing.

Love grows when you are kind and gentle,
when you share your things and your time,
when you take turns and have fun together.

Sometimes, the love you have for things can change.
As you grow up, you can change a little and the
things you love can change.

If the love for your things stops growing,
you can decide that it's time to try some new things.

You can give the things you used to love to someone
else who will love them too.

Sometimes the love you have for others can change.
Sometimes, other people can be a bit mean or they can start loving things that you don't love much.

Your love for those people might stop growing for a while,
but you will still have plenty of love to give to someone else.

Sometimes, the love two grown-ups have can change.

They can stop listening.
They can stop being kind and they can stop doing fun things together.

If the love between two grown-ups stops growing,

they can decide that it is best that they stop sharing their lives together and move to live in different places.

If your grown-ups move into separate places,

the love you might have for your family
doesn't need to stop growing.

Even if the love your grown-ups had for each other has changed, the love you have for each of your grown-ups doesn't have to stop growing.

The love each of your grown-ups has for you doesn't have to stop growing, either.

And if your grown-ups decide to start loving other grown-ups, remember that love doesn't ever have to run out.

Just as a tree continues to grow,
there is plenty of love to share with everyone.

And, if you are ready, there may even be some new things,
and friends and family to love...

and to love you right back.